Stunning Stunts

Written by Samantha Montgomerie

Collins

Stunt artists have a thrilling job!
They screech off in cars and jump
from towers.

They must train hard to act out fights, run at high speeds and jump high.

Stunt artists agree to do stunts so that no one gets hurt.

4

They start by thinking of the risks.
They train to do stunts.

Stunt artists train to get lots of skills. Some train to flee in speeding cars.

Some train to slip down flights of stairs.
Some burst out of speeding trains.

Stunt artists act out fighting sprees.
They flip, kick and punch in street fights.

8

They train to hurl spears. They train to fight so that no one is hurt.

Stunt artists train to float up high.
They swoop in the air.

A hoist lifts the stunt artist up so they can swoop down.

hoist

harness

Stunt artists train hard for years.
They plan stunts to avoid harm.

They screech, speed and burst on to the screen. They are not afraid to do stunning stunts.

Stunning stunts

After reading

Letters and Sounds: Phase 4

Word count: 167

Focus on adjacent consonants with long vowel phonemes, e.g. *swoop*.

Common exception words: have, no, of, one, out, so, some, they, to, do, the, by, are

Curriculum links (National Curriculum, Year 1): Science: Animals, including humans

National Curriculum learning objectives: Reading/word reading: apply phonic knowledge and skills as the route to decode words; read accurately by blending sounds in unfamiliar words containing GPCs that have been taught; read common exception words; read other words of more than one syllable that contain taught GPCs; read aloud accurately books that are consistent with their developing phonic knowledge; Reading/comprehension: link what they have read or hear read to their own experiences; discuss word meanings; discuss the significance of the title and events

Developing fluency

- Discuss the layout of the text and features of the non-fiction book such as headings, labels and captions with your child. Think about how these help the reader to navigate the text.
- Look at the use of punctuation marks such as commas and exclamation marks. Discuss how these affect the expression used when reading aloud.

Phonic practice

- Look through the book together. What words can you find with the adjacent consonant "fl"? (*flee, flights, flip, float*)
- Can your child think of items from around the home/garden/school beginning with the following adjacent consonants? fr, tr, pl, sp, fl, st. (e.g. *fridge, tray, plaster, spoon, flower pot, stairs*)

Extending vocabulary

- Ask your child:
  - What does the word **flee** mean? (e.g. *to escape, run away*)
  - How many words can you think of to use instead of **stunning**? (e.g. *amazing, fantastic, magnificent*)
  - Can you think of a sentence using the word **screech**? (e.g. *the racing car screeched around the corner.*)